The Leap Forward

A DAILY MOTIVATIONAL JOURNAL

GEOFFREY FOOSE

authorHOUSE®

AuthorHouse™
1663 Liberty Drive
Bloomington, IN 47403
www.authorhouse.com
Phone: 1 (800) 839-8640

Published by AuthorHouse 07//15/2016

ISBN: 978-1-5246-1795-0 (sc)
ISBN: 978-1-5246-1796-7 (hc)
ISBN: 978-1-5246-1794-3 (e)

Library of Congress Control Number: 2016911210

Print information available on the last page.

This book is printed on acid-free paper.

ACKNOWLEDGEMENT

The completion of this book could not have been made possible without the participation and assistance of so many people. Their contributions are sincerely appreciated and gratefully acknowledged. The individuals who I would like to express my deepest appreciation for are the following:

Pamela Foose: thank you for endless support and love that you have showed me throughout my life. Also, for your wisdom and talent while assisting me with the layout and format of this publication.

Richard Dewees: thank you for your support and wisdom throughout the process of this book. Your advice and input help make this publication possible.

To all my relatives, friends, and children (Kasey, Caitlyn, and Cameron) who have showed their support to me throughout this process

Thank you

Geoffrey Foose

JANUARY 1

_____

_____

_____

_____

_____

_____

_____

_____

_____

_____

THE RESOLUTIONS
FRESH START FOR NEW BEGINNINGS
GOALS, DREAMS, AND DESIRES

JANUARY 2

LEAD BY EXAMPLE
KNOW THYSELF AND BE THYSELF
THEN STRIVE FOR SUCCESS

JANUARY 3

_____

_____

_____

_____

_____

_____

_____

_____

_____

_____

_____

_____

OPPORTUNITY
TAKING A CHANCE ON SOMETHING
BETTER THAN BEFORE

JANUARY 4

THE ENTREPRENEUR
FAILURE IS NOT AN OPTION
FINANCIAL FREEDOM

JANUARY 5

_____

_____

_____

_____

_____

_____

_____

_____

_____

_____

_____

_____

BREAKING THE PATTERN

THE SCIENCE OF ACHIEVEMENT

THE TRUE COMPONENT

JANUARY 6

SHOW OFF YOUR TALENTS
BECOME THE INSPIRATION
FOR OTHERS TO SEE

JANUARY 7

JANUARY 8

BE INDEPENDENT
BECOME A RISK TAKER AND
WATCH THE REWARDS COME

JANUARY 9

HAVING SPECIAL GIFTS
SHOULD ALWAYS INSPIRE OTHERS
CAN NOT BE WASTED

—[9]—

JANUARY 10

_____

_____

_____

_____

_____

_____

_____

_____

_____

_____

_____

SOMETHING DIFFERENT
BE THE CHANGE YOU WISH TO SEE
POSITIVE OUTCOMES

JANUARY 11

GIVING OF YOURSELF

INTERACTION WITH OTHERS

TOUCHING PEOPLE'S LIVES

JANUARY 12

_____

_____

_____

_____

_____

_____

_____

_____

_____

_____

_____

RESPECTING OTHERS
EQUALS BETTER MANAGEMENT
THAT LEADS TO SUCCESS

JANUARY 13

_____

_____

_____

_____

_____

_____

_____

_____

_____

_____

_____

_____

THINGS IN LIFE WILL CHANGE
IT IS ALWAYS UP TO YOU
IF THINGS GET BETTER

JANUARY 14

_____

_____

_____

_____

_____

_____

_____

_____

_____

_____

_____

PRAYING EVERYDAY

CLARITY AND ABUNDANCE

GREATNESS IS WITHIN

JANUARY 15

_____

_____

_____

_____

_____

_____

_____

_____

_____

_____

_____

_____

KEEP YOUR DREAMS ALIVE

ALWAYS KEEP PUSHING FORWARD

NEVER GIVING UP

JANUARY 16

_____

_____

_____

_____

_____

_____

_____

_____

_____

_____

_____

DETERMINATION
WORKING HARD TOWARDS YOUR GOALS
ALWAYS STAY THE COURSE

JANUARY 17

_____

_____

_____

_____

_____

_____

_____

_____

_____

_____

_____

ALWAYS BE READING
GREAT SOURCE OF KNOWLEDGE
WORDS ARE POWERFUL

JANUARY 18

Build everyone up
By lending a helping hand
Never hold them down

JANUARY 19

WORKING EVERYDAY
HAVING ATTAINABLE GOALS
PRODUCES RESULTS

JANUARY 20

_____

_____

_____

_____

_____

_____

_____

_____

_____

_____

_____

YOU FIRST MUST BELIEVE
YOU ARE CAPABLE OF MORE
BEFORE YOU BEGIN

JANUARY 21

EATING HEALTHIER

ESTABLISHING NEW DIETS

RESTORING ONE'S SELF

JANUARY 22

JANUARY 23

_____

_____

_____

_____

_____

_____

_____

_____

_____

_____

_____

LEND A HELPING HAND
NEVER LOOK DOWN ON SOMEONE
ALWAYS SHOWING LOVE

JANUARY 24

USE YOUR DAILY GIFTS
BE READY FOR ANYTHING
NEVER QUIT TRYING

JANUARY 25

SET YOUR STANDARDS HIGH
BELIEVE THE IMPOSSIBLE
HOLD UNTO YOUR DREAMS

JANUARY 26

_____

_____

_____

_____

_____

_____

_____

_____

_____

_____

_____

THOUGHTS BECOME OUR WORDS
WORDS BECOME SOMEONE'S ACTION
ACTIONS START OUR DREAMS

JANUARY 27

Working everyday
Looking towards our vision
Destiny revealed

JANUARY 28

BE THE SOLUTION
ACTIONS SPEAK LOUDER THAN WORDS
NEVER THE PROBLEM

JANUARY 29

Words match one's action
Can change your circumstance
The right time is now

—[29]—

JANUARY 30

JANUARY 31

_____

_____

_____

_____

_____

_____

_____

_____

_____

_____

_____

_____

KEEP TAKING YOUR TURN
NEXT WORK WILL BE YOUR BEST WORK
KEEP PUSHING FORWARD

FEBRUARY 1

_____

_____

_____

_____

_____

_____

_____

_____

_____

_____

_____

ALWAYS LOVE THYSELF
BE COMMITTED TO YOURSELF
FINDING HAPPINESS

FEBRUARY 2

_____

_____

_____

_____

_____

_____

_____

_____

_____

_____

_____

LEAD BY EXAMPLE
BE THE LIGHT IN THE DARKNESS
ALWAYS SHINING BRIGHT

FEBRUARY 3

_____

_____

_____

_____

_____

_____

_____

_____

_____

_____

_____

SHOWING COMPASSION
GIVING IS NOT A HARD THING
IT IS A HEART THING

FEBRUARY 4

_____

_____

_____

_____

_____

_____

_____

_____

_____

_____

_____

_____

Be the difference
Always doing the right thing
Give unto others

FEBRUARY 5

TAKING BIGGER RISKS
HAVING A POSITIVE OUTLOOK
WILL PRODUCE RESULTS

FEBRUARY 6

_____

_____

_____

_____

_____

_____

_____

_____

_____

_____

_____

_____

_____

BE TRUE TO YOURSELF

RESPECT AND LOVE EVERYONE

KNOW THAT YOU ARE BLESSED

FEBRUARY 7

BUILDING OTHERS UP
SHOWING THAT YOU'RE A LEADER
BRINGS FORTH CHARACTER

FEBRUARY 8

_____

_____

_____

_____

_____

_____

_____

_____

_____

_____

_____

_____

PLAN OUT EVERYDAY
DO WHAT YOU WANT TO DO
ALWAYS MOVE FORWARD

FEBRUARY 9

_____

_____

_____

_____

_____

_____

_____

_____

_____

_____

_____

_____

GIVE UNTO YOURSELF
BE SOMEONE'S INSPIRATION
SHOW THEM THAT YOU CARE

FEBRUARY 10

_____

_____

_____

_____

_____

_____

_____

_____

_____

_____

_____

POSITIVE PEOPLE

IGNORE NEGATIVITY

PUSH THEMSELVES FORWARD

FEBRUARY 11

_____

_____

_____

_____

_____

_____

_____

_____

_____

_____

_____

GRAB A BOOK EACH DAY
LIVE AND ENGAGE IN LEARNING
BECOME A READER

FEBRUARY 12

_____

_____

_____

_____

_____

_____

_____

_____

_____

_____

_____

_____

OPENING OUR HEARTS

HAVING DAILY DEVOTIONS

PREPARING ONE'S MIND

FEBRUARY 13

_____

_____

_____

_____

_____

_____

_____

_____

_____

_____

_____

BECOME ORGANIZED

SET FORTH APPROACHABLE GOALS

DEVELOP A PLAN

FEBRUARY 14

ALWAYS LOVE YOURSELF
BEAUTY COMES FROM WITHIN AND
TRUE PASSION LIVES ON

FEBRUARY 15

DECIDE TO DO MORE

BECOME A FRIEND TO OTHERS

MAKE A DIFFERENCE

FEBRUARY 16

_____

_____

_____

_____

_____

_____

_____

_____

_____

_____

_____

_____

SET YOUR STANDARDS HIGH
COMMIT FULLY TO SOMEONE
LOVE THEM FOREVER

FEBRUARY 17

ESTABLISH GOOD FRIENDS
MAKE YOURSELF AVAILABLE
SUPPORT THEM ALWAYS

FEBRUARY 18

Do not be afraid

All things are made possible

Become courageous

FEBRUARY 19

KEEP YOUR DREAMS ALIVE
YOUR BEST DAYS ARE STILL AHEAD
ALWAYS STAY THE COURSE

FEBRUARY 20

_____

_____

_____

_____

_____

_____

_____

_____

_____

_____

_____

_____

ALWAYS STAY FOCUSED
KEEPING THE EYE ON THE PRIZE
HUMBLE AND STEADFAST

FEBRUARY 21

DREAMS WILL DEFINE US

HARD WORK MAKES DREAMS COME TRUE

KEEP UP THE EFFORT

FEBRUARY 22

Always know your worth
You are the prize worth winning
So wait patiently

FEBRUARY 23

DO OR DO NOT DO

EXCUSES WILL SHOW FAILURE

THERE IS NO TRYING

FEBRUARY 24

FEBRUARY 25

_____

_____

_____

_____

_____

_____

_____

_____

_____

_____

_____

LOVE AND COMPASSION
HELPING OTHERS THROUGH THE STORM
WILL SET YOUR HEART FREE

FEBRUARY 26

GUIDE MY EMOTIONS
FILL ME NOW WITH YOUR PRESENCE
SHOW ME THE RIGHT WAY

FEBRUARY 27

_____

_____

_____

_____

_____

_____

_____

_____

_____

_____

_____

BUILDING CHARACTER
SETTING A GOOD EXAMPLE
KNOWING RIGHT AND WRONG

FEBRUARY 28

_____

_____

_____

_____

_____

_____

_____

_____

_____

_____

_____

_____

GIVING OF OURSELVES
TREAT EVERYONE EQUALLY
SHOWING LOVE ALWAYS

MARCH 1

_____

_____

_____

_____

_____

_____

_____

_____

_____

_____

_____

EVERY STEP FORWARD
WORK TO CHANGE YOUR CIRCUMSTANCE
THE RIGHT TIME IS NOW

MARCH 2

_____

_____

_____

_____

_____

_____

_____

_____

_____

_____

_____

_____

YOU WILL LEARN SOMETHING
BELIEVE IN YOURSELF EVERYDAY
YOU WILL EARN SOMETHING

MARCH 3

_____

_____

_____

_____

_____

_____

_____

_____

_____

_____

_____

PREPARING YOURSELF
GET OUT OF YOUR COMFORT ZONE
WORK HARD DREAM BIGGER

MARCH 4

STEP OUT AND MARCH FORTH
TO YOUR TRUE CALLING IN LIFE
AND CONTINUE ON

MARCH 5

_____

_____

_____

_____

_____

_____

_____

_____

_____

_____

WORDS BECOME ACTIONS

ACTIONS REFLECT LEADERSHIP

LEADERSHIP GUIDES US

MARCH 6

MARCH 7

_____

_____

_____

_____

_____

_____

_____

_____

_____

_____

_____

THOUGHTS TURN TO ACTIONS
FOLLOW YOUR GREAT IDEAS
MAKE IT SOMETHING MORE

MARCH 8

_____

_____

_____

_____

_____

_____

_____

_____

_____

_____

_____

_____

BUILDING PEOPLE UP

ALWAYS PUTTING OTHERS FIRST

HOMEMADE HAPPINESS

MARCH 9

DEVELOPING GROWTH
FEELINGS MAKE AND DEFINE US
AND MAKES US STRONGER

_____

_____

_____

_____

_____

_____

_____

_____

_____

_____

_____

BRAND NEW BEGINNINGS

BRING NEW OPPORTUNITIES

BUILD NEW SOLUTIONS

MARCH 11

_____

_____

_____

_____

_____

_____

_____

_____

_____

_____

_____

_____

TRAIN ACCORDINGLY
TEACH US THE POWER OF YES
INSPIRING OTHERS

MARCH 12

Do not be afraid
To do the impossible
Fear equals failure

MARCH 13

_____

_____

_____

_____

_____

_____

_____

_____

_____

_____

_____

FEAR FREEZES PEOPLE
ENABLES THEM FROM DOING
THEIR CALLING IN LIFE

MARCH 14

Gear up your spirit
Get out and accomplish more
Establish your goals

MARCH 15

_____

_____

_____

_____

_____

_____

_____

_____

_____

_____

_____

BUILDING ON YOUR STRENGTH
SHOWING YOUR DEVELOPMENT
GROWING EVERYDAY

MARCH 16

Successful people

Happier and healthier

Life learning lessons

MARCH 17

BE WORTHY OF WEALTH
KEEP SMILING AND GO FORWARD
AND MAKE YOUR VISION

MARCH 18

Focus on today
Leave yesterday behind you
Start tomorrow new

MARCH 19

_____

_____

_____

_____

_____

_____

_____

_____

_____

_____

NEVER STOP FIGHTING
EVEN WHEN ALL HOPE LOOKS LOST
TAKE THE LEAP FORWARD

MARCH 20

_____

_____

_____

_____

_____

_____

_____

_____

_____

_____

_____

_____

LIFE IS NOT EASY
STEP OUT OF YOUR COMFORT ZONE
CREATE YOUR STORY

MARCH 21

RUN AND SPRING FORWARD
ABUNDANCE WILL FOLLOW YOU
GO AFTER YOUR DREAMS

MARCH 22

_____

_____

_____

_____

_____

_____

_____

_____

_____

_____

_____

ALWAYS STAY FOCUSED

TAKE THE MOMENT TO LISTEN

ALWAYS IMPROVING

MARCH 23

SEASON OF GREATNESS

FIND THE BALANCE IN YOUR LIFE

SUCCESSFUL PEOPLE

MARCH 24

_____

_____

_____

_____

_____

_____

_____

_____

_____

_____

_____

_____

POWERFUL WRITING

PUTTING YOUR THOUGHTS ON PAPER

INSPIRING OTHERS

MARCH 25

_____

_____

_____

_____

_____

_____

_____

_____

_____

_____

_____

ONE SINGLE CHAPTER
OF DEPRESSION AND DESPAIR
SHALL NOT DEFINE YOU

MARCH 26

Be willing to work
Help others to reach their goals
Growing together

MARCH 27

_____

_____

_____

_____

_____

_____

_____

_____

_____

_____

A PLAN OF ACTION
IS A THOUGHT INTO MOTION
WITH AN END RESULT

MARCH 28

_____

_____

_____

_____

_____

_____

_____

_____

_____

_____

_____

_____

NEVER CHASE PEOPLE
WHO ARE NOT MEANT TO BE THERE
ALWAYS LEAVE THEM BEHIND

MARCH 29

NEGATIVITY
WILL TAKE AWAY HAPPINESS
AND LEAVE YOU EMPTY

MARCH 30

_____

_____

_____

_____

_____

_____

_____

_____

_____

_____

_____

GUARD ME AGAINST GREED
KEEPING MY HEART AND THOUGHTS PURE
FULFILL MY SPIRIT

MARCH 31

_____

_____

_____

_____

_____

_____

_____

_____

_____

_____

_____

EVERYONE STRUGGLES
STRUGGLES DOES NOT MEAN FAILURE
ALWAYS FINISH STRONG

APRIL 1

_____

_____

_____

_____

_____

_____

_____

_____

_____

_____

DO NOT BE FOOLISH

ALWAYS WORK TOWARD YOUR GOALS

BECOME DILIGENT

APRIL 2

LISTEN TO YOUR HEART
TAKE RISKS AND PREPARE YOUR LIFE
BECOME PRODUCTIVE

TRUST TAKES YEARS TO BUILD
MATTER OF SECONDS TO BREAK
FOREVER TO FIX

APRIL 4

APRIL 5

FIGHT FOR YOUR VISION
BECOME PRODUCTIVE YET CALM
STAND UP FOR YOUR DREAMS

APRIL 6

NEVER STOP TRYING
TOUGH TIMES CREATE TOUGH PEOPLE
BE THAT COMEBACK KID

_____

_____

_____

_____

_____

_____

_____

_____

_____

_____

LISTEN TO YOUR HEART
ALWAYS BE HUMBLE AND STRONG
STAY TRUE TO YOURSELF

APRIL 8

_____

_____

_____

_____

_____

_____

_____

_____

_____

_____

_____

CLEAR YOUR EMOTIONS
DO NOT POLLUTE YOUR MINDSET
YOU DESERVE BETTER

SUPPORTING YOUR FRIENDS
ALWAYS GIVE A HELPING HAND
PUTTING OTHERS FIRST

APRIL 10

_____

_____

_____

_____

_____

_____

_____

_____

_____

_____

BELIEVE IN YOURSELF
YOU ARE HAPPY AND HEALTHY
YOU CAN DO ANYTHING

APRIL 11

_____

_____

_____

_____

_____

_____

_____

_____

_____

_____

_____

BE HUMBLE AND STRONG
BE A LIGHT UNTO OTHERS
ALWAYS SHOWING LOVE

APRIL 12

BRAND NEW TOMORROWS
BRING NEW OPPORTUNITIES
TO START OVER NEW

_____

_____

_____

_____

_____

_____

_____

_____

_____

_____

_____

PROVIDE FOR OTHERS
GIVE UNCONDITIONALLY
HAVE A LOVING HEART

APRIL 14

_____

_____

_____

_____

_____

_____

_____

_____

_____

_____

_____

KNOW WHEN TO GIVE PRAISE
NEVER CRITICIZE OTHERS
FOR YOUR SAME MISTAKES

APRIL 15

Change your perspective
Put a plan into action
Create daily goals

APRIL 16

_____

_____

_____

_____

_____

_____

_____

_____

_____

_____

_____

WANT MORE FROM YOURSELF
DEVELOP A NEW OUTLOOK
HAVE A PLAN IN PLACE

APRIL 17

_____

_____

_____

_____

_____

_____

_____

_____

_____

_____

_____

BEGIN SOMETHING NEW
SHOW OFF YOUR ABILITY
START A CHANGE IN YOU

APRIL 18

_____

_____

_____

_____

_____

_____

_____

_____

_____

_____

HAVE STRENGTH AND POWER
COUNT YOUR AMAZING BLESSINGS
SHOW OFF YOUR GREATNESS

APRIL 19

Leave your comfort zone
You are meant for so much more
Always leap forward

APRIL 20

_____

_____

_____

_____

_____

_____

_____

_____

_____

_____

_____

ALWAYS BE YOURSELF
DON'T LOSE YOUR TRUE POTENTIAL
BY WEARING A MASK

APRIL 21

_____

_____

_____

_____

_____

_____

_____

_____

_____

_____

_____

DISCOVER YOUR WORTH

APPRECIATE ONE'S VALUE

WEALTH COMES FROM WITHIN

APRIL 22

_____

_____

_____

_____

_____

_____

_____

_____

_____

_____

_____

MAKE EVERYDAY COUNT
TOMORROW IS NOT PROMISED
IT BEGINS WITH YOU

APRIL 23

Have better insight
Evaluate your new life
Through peace and blessings

APRIL 24

NEVER JUDGE PEOPLE
EVERYONE HAS A CERTAIN PAST
JUST TELL YOUR STORY

APRIL 25

_____

_____

_____

_____

_____

_____

_____

_____

_____

_____

_____

MAKE A DIFFERENCE
BE THE CHANGE YOU WISH TO SEE
SEEING IS BELIEVING

APRIL 26

_____

_____

_____

_____

_____

_____

_____

_____

_____

_____

_____

MAKE GREAT DECISIONS
BECOME NURTURING AND KIND
TAKE THE TIME TO GIVE

APRIL 27

_____

_____

_____

_____

_____

_____

_____

_____

_____

_____

_____

BECOME A SERVANT
HELPING THE COMMUNITY
ALWAYS GIVING BACK

APRIL 28

IF YOU DO NOTHING
THERE WILL BE NO END RESULT
SO DO SOMETHING NOW

APRIL 29

_____

_____

_____

_____

_____

_____

_____

_____

_____

_____

_____

CREATE YOUR FUTURE
NEVER RISK BEING HAPPY
GO AFTER YOUR DREAMS

APRIL 30

_____

_____

_____

_____

_____

_____

_____

_____

_____

_____

NEVER COMPROMISE
OUR TRUE DESIRE FOR SUCCESS
CAN NOT BE MEASURED

MAY 1

_____

_____

_____

_____

_____

_____

_____

_____

_____

_____

_____

MAKE THE TIME TO HELP
EVERYONE THAT IS IN NEED
PUTTING YOUR FRIENDS FIRST

MAY 2

Always take the chance
To achieve your thoughts and dreams
Believe in yourself

—[122]—

_____

_____

_____

_____

_____

_____

_____

_____

_____

_____

SOMETIMES LIFE HAPPENS
TAKE COURAGE TO KEEP GOING
GIVING UP IS FINAL

MAY 4

_____

_____

_____

_____

_____

_____

_____

_____

_____

_____

_____

WINNERS KEEP GOING
LEARNING FROM THEIR PAST MISTAKES
IMPROVING THEIR WAYS

MAY 5

_____

_____

_____

_____

_____

_____

_____

_____

_____

_____

_____

SUPPORT THOSE IN NEED
TAKE THE TIME TO HELP OTHERS
MAKING THINGS BETTER

MAY 6

NO ONE IS PERFECT
EVERYONE HAS FAULTS AND FLAWS
IMPROVING ONE'S SELF

MAY 7

DO NOT LET THE PAST
DISCOURAGE YOU FROM TRYING
MOVE FORWARD IN LIFE

MAY 8

_____

_____

_____

_____

_____

_____

_____

_____

_____

_____

GOOD RELATIONSHIPS
WILL NOT DRAG A PERSON DOWN
JUST MAKE THEM STRONGER

_____

_____

_____

_____

_____

_____

_____

_____

_____

_____

_____

SHOW THEM THE RIGHT WAY
NEVER LET A FRIEND STRUGGLE
GIVE THEM YOUR SUPPORT

MAY 10

FAITH IS TRUSTING GOD
THAT EVERYTHING WILL WORK OUT
BETTER THAN BEFORE

MAY 11

THE BEST THINGS IN LIFE
ARE NEVER THINGS BUT PEOPLE
SO MAKE THEM FEEL LOVED

MAY 12

_____

_____

_____

_____

_____

_____

_____

_____

_____

_____

HAVE A STRUCTURED PLAN
NEVER CREATE YOUR VISION
WITHOUT PLANNING FIRST

MAY 13

_____

_____

_____

_____

_____

_____

_____

_____

_____

_____

_____

BE AVAILABLE
HONOR AND LIVE FOR OTHERS
SHOWING THEM THE WAY

MAY 14

_____

_____

_____

_____

_____

_____

_____

_____

_____

_____

_____

SHOW HER THAT YOU CARE
A MOTHER'S LOVE IS ENDLESS
SO ALWAYS LOVE HER

MAY 15

Maintain a structure
Have strong communication
Become discipline

MAY 16

_____

_____

_____

_____

_____

_____

_____

_____

_____

_____

ALWAYS BE HONEST
NEVER LIE OR KEEP SECRETS
FROM THE ONE'S WE LOVE

_____

_____

_____

_____

_____

_____

_____

_____

_____

_____

_____

CHEER EVERYONE ON
SHOW THEM THEY ARE NOT ALONE
ALWAYS HAVE THEIR BACK

MAY 18

_____

_____

_____

_____

_____

_____

_____

_____

_____

_____

_____

HELPING THOSE IN NEED
INSPIRES YOU TO BE BETTER
IN EVERYDAY LIFE

_____

_____

_____

_____

_____

_____

_____

_____

_____

_____

_____

DON'T DWELL ON PAYDAY
BE FINANCIALLY SECURE
THROUGH DAILY HARD WORK

MAY 20

_____

_____

_____

_____

_____

_____

_____

_____

_____

_____

KNOW THAT YOU ARE BLESSED
BECOME PROUD OF WHO YOU ARE
AND WHO YOU WILL BE

MAY 21

_____

_____

_____

_____

_____

_____

_____

_____

_____

_____

_____

THE LENGTH OF FRIENDSHIP
DOESN'T DETERMINE LOYALTY
HAVING THEIR BACK DOES

MAY 22

———————————————————————————

———————————————————————————

———————————————————————————

———————————————————————————

———————————————————————————

———————————————————————————

———————————————————————————

———————————————————————————

———————————————————————————

———————————————————————————

BECOME A LEADER

HAVE RESPONSIBILITIES

TEACH AND TRAIN OTHERS

MAY 23

_____

_____

_____

_____

_____

_____

_____

_____

_____

_____

_____

SET YOUR MIND ON THINGS
THAT ARE MUCH GREATER THAN YOU
THE KEYS TO SUCCESS

MAY 24

_____

_____

_____

_____

_____

_____

_____

_____

_____

_____

THE SUN WILL SHINE BRIGHT
IT NEVER RAINS FOREVER
CLEAR SKIES ARE COMING

MAY 25

_____

_____

_____

_____

_____

_____

_____

_____

_____

_____

_____

BE STRONG EVERYDAY

THE ROAD IS A LONG JOURNEY

THINGS WILL GET BETTER

MAY 26

NEVER STOP TRYING
SOMETHING BETTER AWAITS YOU
YOU'RE A CHAMPION

MAY 27

I AM DETERMINED

I WILL NOT LOSE OR GIVE UP

I WILL TRY AGAIN

MAY 28

_____

_____

_____

_____

_____

_____

_____

_____

_____

_____

_____

BE THE DIFFERENCE
THROUGH HONESTY AND RESPECT
SHOW OTHERS THE LIGHT

MAY 29

NEVER BE A LIAR
LYING CAUSES SUFFERING
ALWAYS TELL THE TRUTH

MAY 30

_____

_____

_____

_____

_____

_____

_____

_____

_____

_____

_____

THE CIRCLE OF FRIENDS
SHOULD BE BASED ON QUALITY
NEVER QUANTITY

MAY 31

_____

_____

_____

_____

_____

_____

_____

_____

_____

_____

BELIEVE IN YOUR FRIENDS
SHOWING THEM LOVE AND SUPPORT
HELPING THEM ALWAYS

JUNE 1

_____

_____

_____

_____

_____

_____

_____

_____

_____

_____

BREAKING THE HABIT
NEEDING TO MAKE A NEW CHANGE
HAVING A FRESH START

JUNE 2

_____

_____

_____

_____

_____

_____

_____

_____

_____

_____

_____

HAVING A CLOSED MIND
WILL NEVER BRING UPON A
POSITIVE RESULT

JUNE 3

_____

_____

_____

_____

_____

_____

_____

_____

_____

_____

GO AFTER YOUR DREAMS
NO MATTER HOW TOUGH LIFE GETS
YOU ARE MEANT FOR MORE

JUNE 4

LIFE IS WAY TOO SHORT
DO NOT HESITATE OR WAIT
CREATE SOMETHING NEW

JUNE 5

CHANGE YOUR CHARACTER
BE THE CHANGE YOU WISH TO SEE
AND SHOW THE NEW YOU

JUNE 6

Always remember
Obstacles can not crush me
Just make me stronger

JUNE 7

_____

_____

_____

_____

_____

_____

_____

_____

_____

_____

_____

WAKE UP AND GET DRESSED
YOUR PRESENT SITUATION
IMPROVES EVERYDAY

JUNE 8

BREATHE AND MOVE FORWARD
DON'T LET OTHERS STEAL YOUR DREAMS
HARD WORK WILL PAY OFF

JUNE 9

WHAT DOES NOT KILL YOU
CAN ONLY MAKE YOU STRONGER
OVERCOMING LIFE

THE THREE PRINCIPLES

DO GOOD, LIVE WELL, AND LOVE LIFE

LIVING POSITIVE

JUNE 11

_____

_____

_____

_____

_____

_____

_____

_____

_____

_____

IT IS NOT THE END
DON'T STRESS YOURSELF OUT TOO MUCH
LIFE WILL GET BETTER

JUNE 12

_____

_____

_____

_____

_____

_____

_____

_____

_____

_____

BECOME A SERVANT
BE SOMETHING BIGGER THAN YOU
SO OTHERS WILL SEE

JUNE 13

JUNE 14

FIGHTING TO BE YOU

INTERACTING ON YOUR OWN

BE YOUR OWN LEGEND

JUNE 15

_____

_____

_____

_____

_____

_____

_____

_____

_____

_____

THERE IS A BRIGHT LIGHT
AT THE END OF EACH TUNNEL
SO KEEP IT MOVING

JUNE 16

NEVER CHANGE YOURSELF
WALK IN THE PATH OF GREATNESS
AND NEVER LOOK BACK

JUNE 17

_____

_____

_____

_____

_____

_____

_____

_____

_____

_____

CONCENTRATE ON YOU
HELP YOUR FRIENDS AND FAMILY
AND EVERYONE ELSE

JUNE 18

_____

_____

_____

_____

_____

_____

_____

_____

_____

_____

_____

BE THE TYPE OF MAN
THAT WOMEN LOVE AND ADMIRE
AND CHILDREN ADORE

JUNE 19

_____

_____

_____

_____

_____

_____

_____

_____

_____

_____

_____

RISE UP AND START FRESH
SEE THE OPPORTUNITY
IN EVERY NEW DAY

JUNE 20

_____

_____

_____

_____

_____

_____

_____

_____

_____

_____

EVERY JOURNEY STARTS
BY MAKING A DECISION
TO TAKE THAT FIRST STEP

JUNE 21

_____

_____

_____

_____

_____

_____

_____

_____

_____

_____

_____

THE START OF SUMMER
ALLOWS EVERYONE TO SHINE
BIGGER AND BRIGHTER

JUNE 22

_____

_____

_____

_____

_____

_____

_____

_____

_____

_____

_____

ONE'S MOTIVATION
DETERMINES WHAT PEOPLE DO
SO BECOME FOCUSED

JUNE 23

_____

_____

_____

_____

_____

_____

_____

_____

_____

_____

_____

THE ABILITY
IS ONE'S CAPABILITY
OF DOING THINGS RIGHT

JUNE 24

_____

_____

_____

_____

_____

_____

_____

_____

_____

_____

A PERSON'S FUTURE
IS CREATED BY WHAT YOU
ACCOMPLISH TODAY

JUNE 25

_____

_____

_____

_____

_____

_____

_____

_____

_____

_____

_____

IT'S NEVER TOO LATE
KEEP WORKING TOWARDS YOUR GOALS
ALWAYS PUSH YOURSELF

JUNE 26

_____

_____

_____

_____

_____

_____

_____

_____

_____

_____

_____

ACCEPT WHAT IS GOOD

LET GO OF THE NEGATIVES

HAVE YOUR FAITH RESTORED

JUNE 27

_____

_____

_____

_____

_____

_____

_____

_____

_____

_____

EVERYBODY FAILS
FAILURE IS NOT FALLING DOWN
IT'S NOT GETTING UP

JUNE 28

JUNE 29

BE WILLING TO RISK
SETTLING FOR ORDINARY
IS NOT AN OPTION

JUNE 30

_____

_____

_____

_____

_____

_____

_____

_____

_____

_____

_____

PEOPLE WHO SUCCEED
HAVE DRIVE AND MOMENTUM TO
ACCOMPLISH MORE

JULY 1

_____

_____

_____

_____

_____

_____

_____

_____

_____

_____

BE KIND AND HELPFUL
TREAT ALL PEOPLE WITH RESPECT
THEY ALL DESERVE IT

JULY 2

_____

_____

_____

_____

_____

_____

_____

_____

_____

_____

_____

THE MEANING OF LIFE
IS TO DISCOVER YOUR GIFTS
AND GIVE IT AWAY

JULY 3

_____

_____

_____

_____

_____

_____

_____

_____

_____

_____

_____

PUT YOUR MIND TO IT
ANYTHING IS POSSIBLE
MIND OVER MATTER

JULY 4

_____

_____

_____

_____

_____

_____

_____

_____

_____

_____

FREEDOM IS NOT FREE
HONOR OUR MILITARY
FOR PROTECTING US

JULY 5

_____

_____

_____

_____

_____

_____

_____

_____

_____

_____

_____

BE YOURSELF ALWAYS
STAND OUT AND NEVER FIT IN
BE ORIGINAL

JULY 6

_____

_____

_____

_____

_____

_____

_____

_____

_____

_____

_____

EXCITEMENT AWAITS
WHEN YOU UNLEASH YOURSELF TO
YOUR FULL POTENTIAL

JULY 7

Your next adventure
Should trial and challenge you
To be your very best

JULY 8

_____

_____

_____

_____

_____

_____

_____

_____

_____

_____

THE BIGGEST CHALLENGE
A PERSON WILL FACE IN LIFE
IS FACING THEMSELVES

JULY 9

_____

LIFE IS WAY TOO SHORT
CUT OUT NEGATIVITY
LEAVE IT ALL BEHIND

JULY 10

LEAVE YOUR PAST HABITS
SAYING GOODBYE WILL BE HARD
BUT NECESSARY

JULY 11

_____

_____

_____

_____

_____

_____

_____

_____

_____

_____

SPEND TIME WITH PEOPLE
WHO ARE ALWAYS THERE FOR YOU
SHOWING YOU SUPPORT

JULY 12

JULY 13

_____

_____

_____

_____

_____

_____

_____

_____

_____

_____

_____

TODAY IS RICH WITH
OPPORTUNITIES FOR YOU
TAKE THEM WILLINGLY

JULY 14

Don't let your struggles
Become your identity
Be ready to fight

JULY 15

BECOME COURAGEOUS
FIGHT THROUGH ALL OF YOUR BATTLES
CONSTANTLY WINNING

JULY 16

_____

_____

_____

_____

_____

_____

_____

_____

_____

_____

_____

THE DARKNESS OF DAYS
IS OFTEN THE BRIDGE TO THE
BRIGHTEST TOMORROWS

JULY 17

_____

_____

_____

_____

_____

_____

_____

_____

_____

_____

_____

YESTERDAY IS GONE
DON'T WAIT UNTIL TOMORROW
START SOMETHING TODAY

JULY 18

ALWAYS MOVE FORWARD
KEEP MOVING DOWN THE RIGHT PATH
NEVER LOOKING BACK

JULY 19

_____

_____

_____

_____

_____

_____

_____

_____

_____

_____

_____

CHASE AFTER YOUR DREAMS
FUN AND ADVENTURE AWAITS
SO DON'T HESITATE

JULY 20

EXPLORE YOUR OPTIONS
DECIDE WHAT IS BEST FOR YOU
AND MAKE IT HAPPEN

JULY 21

_____

_____

_____

_____

_____

_____

_____

_____

_____

_____

WORKING SHOULD NEVER
BE YOUR ONLY ADVENTURE
MAKE LIFE FUN AGAIN

JULY 22

_____

_____

_____

_____

_____

_____

_____

_____

_____

_____

THE TRUTH WILL ALWAYS
NO MATTER WHAT YOU DO WILL
COME OUT IN THE END

JULY 23

KNOWING THAT THE RISK
IS GREATER THAN THE AWARD
BECOMES OUR REASON

JULY 24

_____

_____

_____

_____

_____

_____

_____

_____

_____

_____

_____

OUR ADVENTURES
ARE THE ONE'S WE ARE WILLING
TO CASH IN DAILY

JULY 25

_____

_____

_____

_____

_____

_____

_____

_____

_____

_____

DON'T GET SO BUSY
MAKING A LIVING THAT YOU
MISS OUT ON YOUR LIFE

JULY 26

_____

_____

_____

_____

_____

_____

_____

_____

_____

_____

WAKE UP AND SMILE BIG
IT IS FREE FOR EVERYONE
BRIGHTEN SOMEONE'S DAY

JULY 27

Begin where you are
Take what you have learned each day
And apply it now

—{208}—

JULY 28

_____

_____

_____

_____

_____

_____

_____

_____

_____

_____

_____

_____

BE FULL OF PASSION

GIVE UNTO OTHERS FREELY

LET YOUR SPIRIT SHINE

JULY 29

_____

_____

_____

_____

_____

_____

_____

_____

_____

_____

AIM HIGH, WORK HARDER
EXCITING THINGS WILL HAPPEN
IF YOU BELIEVE

JULY 30

_____

_____

_____

_____

_____

_____

_____

_____

_____

_____

_____

MAKE A DECISION
TO WORK EVERYDAY ON THE
GOALS SET FOR YOURSELF

JULY 31

_____

_____

_____

_____

_____

_____

_____

_____

_____

_____

_____

MAKING AN IMPACT
WHAT YOU THINK YOU CAN ACHIEVE
ALWAYS BELIEVING

AUGUST 1

PEOPLE WILL DOUBT YOU
DON'T GIVE IN TO EXCUSES
GO AND PROVE THEM WRONG

AUGUST 2

_____

_____

_____

_____

_____

_____

_____

_____

_____

_____

_____

RUN FAST DO NOT WALK
TOWARDS YOUR THOUGHTS, GOALS, AND DREAMS
NEVER GIVING UP

AUGUST 3

WE CAN'T BE SELFISH
AND NOT FIGHT TO HELP OTHERS
WHEN THEY ARE IN NEED

AUGUST 4

PEOPLE WILL NEVER
FORGET HOW YOU TREAT THEM
SO TREAT THEM KINDLY

AUGUST 5

DO NOT DO WHAT YOU
HAVE ALWAYS DONE IN YOUR LIFE
SHOOT FOR SOMETHING BETTER

AUGUST 6

_____

_____

_____

_____

_____

_____

_____

_____

_____

_____

ALWAYS LIVE YOUR LIFE
TO THE FULLEST BY SHOWING
COURAGE, STRENGTH, AND LOVE

AUGUST 7

_____

_____

_____

_____

_____

_____

_____

_____

_____

_____

_____

COURAGE WITHIN YOU
BE STRONG NEVER GIVE UP
SHOWING BRAVERY

AUGUST 8

ALWAYS BE YOURSELF
HAVE PEOPLE BE PROUD OF YOU
MEANS THAT YOU ARE LOVED

AUGUST 9

_____

_____

_____

_____

_____

_____

_____

_____

_____

_____

WHEN LEAPING FORWARD
ALWAYS REMEMBER IT WILL
BE WORTH THE EFFORT

AUGUST 10

ESTEEM FOR YOURSELF
COMES FROM PUSHING YOURSELF
THROUGH DIFFICULT TIMES

AUGUST 11

PUSH YOURSELF AND GRIND
MAKE A NEW TOMORROW WHILE
STAYING POSITIVE

AUGUST 12

_____

_____

_____

_____

_____

_____

_____

_____

_____

_____

LOVE YOURSELF ENOUGH
TO ALWAYS TRY YOUR HARDEST
EACH AND EVERY DAY

AUGUST 13

_____

_____

_____

_____

_____

_____

_____

_____

_____

_____

_____

YOU'RE ALLOWED TO SCREAM
AND GET FRUSTRATED AND CRY
JUST NEVER GIVE UP

AUGUST 14

_____

_____

_____

_____

_____

_____

_____

_____

_____

_____

DO YOUR BEST DAILY
STOP WORRYING AND LET GO
ALL THINGS WILL WORK OUT

AUGUST 15

BECOME PASSIONATE
ALWAYS HELP AND SERVE OTHERS
BE A GOOD SERVANT

AUGUST 16

_____

_____

_____

_____

_____

_____

_____

_____

_____

_____

HAVING A GOOD HEART
MEANS THAT YOU PUT OTHERS FIRST
INSTEAD OF YOURSELF

AUGUST 17

_____

_____

_____

_____

_____

_____

_____

_____

_____

_____

_____

NEW CHOICES TODAY
WILL BEGIN YOUR NEW JOURNEY
SO CHOOSE THEM WISELY

AUGUST 18

TURN YOUR THOUGHTS INTO
WORDS WHICH WILL TURN TO ACTIONS
WHICH FORMS NEW HABITS

AUGUST 19

_____

_____

_____

_____

_____

_____

_____

_____

_____

_____

_____

ALWAYS KEEP SMILING
NO MATTER HOW BAD LIFE GETS
THINGS WILL GET BETTER

AUGUST 20

_____

_____

_____

_____

_____

_____

_____

_____

_____

_____

AIM TO BE BETTER
WORK ON BECOMING THE BEST
GROWING EVERYDAY

AUGUST 21

IN THE VERY END
WE ONLY REGRET CHANCES
THAT WE DID NOT TAKE

AUGUST 22

BE SILLY BE KIND
GIVE UNTO YOURSELF ALWAYS
HELPING THOSE IN NEED

AUGUST 23

BE A BORN LEADER
ALWAYS GUIDE EVERYONE IN
THE RIGHT DIRECTION

AUGUST 24

BE PEACEFUL, BE STILL
YOUR PERSONAL STORM WILL NOT
LAST YOU FOREVER

AUGUST 25

Don't hide your story
Tell your testimony for
Everyone to hear

AUGUST 26

_____

_____

_____

_____

_____

_____

_____

_____

_____

_____

_____

HAPPY PEOPLE CAUSE
POSITIVE ENERGY TO
RUB OFF ON OTHERS

AUGUST 27

You won't be at peace
Until you learn to move on
From negative things

AUGUST 28

_____

_____

_____

_____

_____

_____

_____

_____

_____

_____

_____

HELP A PERSON SEE
ALL THEIR MAGIC AND REMIND
THEM WHERE TO FIND IT

AUGUST 29

SURROUND YOURSELF WITH
AMAZING FRIENDS THAT LOVE YOU
AND NEVER LEAVE YOU

AUGUST 30

_____

_____

_____

_____

_____

_____

_____

_____

_____

_____

IF YOU IMAGINE
SOMETHING BETTER FOR YOURSELF
YOU CAN CREATE IT

AUGUST 31

HAVE THE ENDURANCE
TO CONSTANTLY BE MOVING
FORWARD IN YOUR LIFE

SEPTEMBER 1

_____

_____

_____

_____

_____

_____

_____

_____

_____

_____

WALK AWAY FROM THOSE
WHO ALWAYS LOOK FOR CONFLICT
IT'S THEIR FIGHT NOT YOURS

SEPTEMBER 2

GOOD THINGS TAKE TIME TO
DEVELOP INTO SOMETHING
GREATER THAN BEFORE

SEPTEMBER 3

MAKE A TRADITION
TO SPEND MORE TIME WITH PEOPLE
YOU CARE FOR THE MOST

SEPTEMBER 4

THE END OF SUMMER
TIME NOW TO RELAX AND CHEER
LABOR DAY IS HERE

SEPTEMBER 5

DON'T LET YOUR TALENTS
GO TO WASTE BECAUSE SOMEONE
DIDN'T BELIEVE IN YOU

SEPTEMBER 6

_____

_____

_____

_____

_____

_____

_____

_____

_____

_____

CHANGE IS ALWAYS HARD
BUT IT ALLOWS A PERSON
TO BE SOMETHING MORE

SEPTEMBER 7

_____

_____

_____

_____

_____

_____

_____

_____

_____

_____

A PARENT IS THE
MOST VALUABLE PERSON
IN ANY CHILD'S LIFE

SEPTEMBER 8

_____

_____

_____

_____

_____

_____

_____

_____

_____

_____

_____

WITHOUT A STRUGGLE
A PERSON WOULD NOT STUMBLE
ACROSS THEIR TRUE STRENGTH

SEPTEMBER 9

EVERYTHING YOU ARE
GOING THROUGH WILL PREPARE YOU
FOR SOMETHING GREATER

SEPTEMBER 10

A FOOL REFUSES
TO LISTEN TO COUNSEL BUT
HEARS AN IDIOT

SEPTEMBER 11

STANDING TOGETHER

REMEMBERING THE FALLEN

UNITED WE STAND

SEPTEMBER 12

WHEN LIFE BECOMES HARD
HAVE FAITH THAT EVERYTHING WILL
WORK OUT FOR THE BEST

SEPTEMBER 13

_____

_____

_____

_____

_____

_____

_____

_____

_____

_____

LIFE IS A JOURNEY
TAKE EACH DAY AT A TIME AND
FOLLOW THE RIGHT PATH

SEPTEMBER 14

_____

_____

_____

_____

_____

_____

_____

_____

_____

_____

DO NOT STOP SHINING
THE WORLD NEEDS TO SEE YOUR LIGHT
TO HELP GUIDE OTHERS

SEPTEMBER 15

_____

_____

_____

_____

_____

_____

_____

_____

_____

_____

_____

TO BE A WINNER
YOU MUST BELIEVE IN YOURSELF
WHEN NO ONE ELSE DOES

SEPTEMBER 16

RISE UP AND START FRESH
SEE THE OPPORTUNITY
WITH EVERY NEW DAY

SEPTEMBER 17

_____

_____

_____

_____

_____

_____

_____

_____

_____

_____

_____

DETERMINATION
IS THE HUMAN WAKE UP CALL
THAT WE MUST ANSWER

SEPTEMBER 18

YOU WILL HAVE TO FIGHT
THROUGH THE BAD DAYS IN ORDER
TO SEE THE BEST DAYS

SEPTEMBER 19

_____

_____

_____

_____

_____

_____

_____

_____

_____

NOTHING WORTH HAVING
COMES EASY TO ANYONE
ALL THINGS TAKE EFFORT

SEPTEMBER 20

_____

_____

_____

_____

_____

_____

_____

_____

_____

_____

IF YOU CAN DREAM IT
MAKE IT YOUR REALITY
AND PROVE OTHERS WRONG

SEPTEMBER 21

_____

_____

_____

_____

_____

_____

_____

_____

_____

_____

_____

DON'T FALL BACK INTO
YOUR SAME HORRIBLE HABITS
MAKE NEW AMAZING ONES

SEPTEMBER 22

CHANGING OF THE LEAVES
SHOULD INSPIRE EVERYONE TO
SEE THE CHANGE IN YOU

SEPTEMBER 23

SAYING I'M SORRY
MEANS ABSOLUTELY NOTHING
IF CHANGE DOESN'T OCCUR

SEPTEMBER 24

_____

_____

_____

_____

_____

_____

_____

_____

_____

_____

_____

HITTING ROCK BOTTOM
IS ONLY CHALLENGING YOU
TO NEVER GIVE UP

SEPTEMBER 25

_____

_____

_____

_____

_____

_____

_____

_____

_____

_____

EVERY STEP UP IS
EXCITING AND DIFFICULT
SO NEVER LOOK BACK

SEPTEMBER 26

_____

_____

_____

_____

_____

_____

_____

_____

_____

_____

_____

No limitations
Means having the freedom to
Accomplish your goals

SEPTEMBER 27

_____

_____

_____

_____

_____

_____

_____

_____

_____

_____

_____

START SOMETHING NEW
CHANGES ARE NEVER EASY
BUT NEITHER IS LIFE

SEPTEMBER 28

_____

_____

_____

_____

_____

_____

_____

_____

_____

_____

GIVE OF YOURSELF BY
SHOWING LOVE AND COMPASSION
EVERY DAY AND NIGHT

SEPTEMBER 29

CHANGE YOUR ATTITUDE
ALWAYS CHOOSE HAPPINESS AND
MAKE YOUR DREAMS COME TRUE

SEPTEMBER 30

_____

_____

_____

_____

_____

_____

_____

_____

_____

_____

_____

ALWAYS TRY YOUR BEST
NEVER MAKE EXCUSES FOR
YOUR LACK OF EFFORT

OCTOBER 1

ALWAYS STAY FOCUSED
CONCENTRATE ON ONE THING AT
ANY GIVEN TIME

OCTOBER 2

Make a solid plan
Set your goals, not to high but
Where you can reach them

OCTOBER 3

IF YOU STAY READY
YOU WON'T HAVE TO GET READY
TO TAKE THE NEXT STEP

OCTOBER 4

_____

_____

_____

_____

_____

_____

_____

_____

_____

_____

_____

MAKE A DECISION
TO MANAGE YOUR OWN AFFAIRS
AND FOLLOW THEM THROUGH

OCTOBER 5

_____

_____

_____

_____

_____

_____

_____

_____

_____

_____

_____

HAVING A PURPOSE
MEANS TAKE DIRECTION IN LIFE
TO WORK ON YOUR DREAMS

OCTOBER 6

_____

_____

_____

_____

_____

_____

_____

_____

_____

_____

_____

HAPPINESS COMES WHEN
YOU BRING PEACE INTO YOUR HEART
AND REWARD YOURSELF

OCTOBER 7

_____

_____

_____

_____

_____

_____

_____

_____

_____

_____

AIM TO HELP YOUR FRIENDS
BEING A GOOD FRIEND TAKES HEART
SO ALWAYS MAKE TIME

OCTOBER 8

_____

WAKE UP EACH MORNING
SEEK WAYS TO MAKE LIFE BETTER
FOR THOSE AROUND YOU

OCTOBER 9

_____

_____

_____

_____

_____

_____

_____

_____

_____

_____

YOUR BELIEFS DO NOT
MAKE YOU A BETTER PERSON
YOUR BEHAVIOR DOES

OCTOBER 10

_____

_____

_____

_____

_____

_____

_____

_____

_____

_____

EVERYTHING YOU DO
DOESN'T NEED TO BE MADE PUBLIC
SO KEEP THINGS PRIVATE

OCTOBER 11

_____

_____

_____

_____

_____

_____

_____

_____

_____

_____

_____

DO NOT LOSE YOUR FAITH
REMEMBER THE ENEMY
WILL ALWAYS TEST YOU

OCTOBER 12

ALWAYS REMAIN STRONG
LIFE HAPPENS FOR A REASON
CONTINUE FIGHTING

OCTOBER 13

BELIEVE IN YOURSELF
RECOGNIZE YOUR OWN PROGRESS
REGARDLESS HOW SMALL

OCTOBER 14

FOCUS ON THINGS
YOU ALREADY HAVE AND THE
THINGS THAT YOU WILL NEED

OCTOBER 15

_____

_____

_____

_____

_____

_____

_____

_____

_____

_____

YOU HAVE THREE CHOICES
GIVE UP IN LIFE OR GIVE IN
OR GIVE IT YOUR ALL

OCTOBER 16

HAVE A HEART OF GOLD
BE THERE FOR OTHERS ALWAYS
HELPING THOSE IN NEED

OCTOBER 17

_____

_____

_____

_____

_____

_____

_____

_____

_____

_____

_____

WHEN LIFE GETS YOU DOWN
CONTROL THE WAY YOU RESPOND
DON'T OVER REACT

OCTOBER 18

_____

_____

_____

_____

_____

_____

_____

_____

_____

_____

_____

PREPARE YOURSELF TO
GET UP, DRESS UP, AND SHOW UP
AND NEVER GIVE UP

OCTOBER 19

HAPPINESS IS NOT
ABOUT GETTING WHAT YOU WANT
BUT WHAT YOU HAVE NOW

OCTOBER 20

_____

_____

_____

_____

_____

_____

_____

_____

_____

_____

BELIEVE IN YOURSELF
KNOW THAT YOU ARE CAPABLE
AND REMOVE ALL DOUBT

OCTOBER 21

_____

_____

_____

_____

_____

_____

_____

_____

_____

_____

IF IT DOESN'T CHALLENGE
YOU BODY, MIND, OR SPIRIT
IT CAN NOT CHANGE YOU

OCTOBER 22

_____

_____

_____

_____

_____

_____

_____

_____

_____

_____

No more needing more
Right now I'm more than enough
And that is okay

OCTOBER 23

LIFE IS NOT ABOUT
DISCOVERING YOURSELF BUT
CREATING YOURSELF

OCTOBER 24

_____

_____

_____

_____

_____

_____

_____

_____

_____

_____

THINGS YOU WANT FROM LIFE
WILL NOT COME SO EASY BUT
THEY WILL BE WORTH IT

OCTOBER 25

_____

_____

_____

_____

_____

_____

_____

_____

_____

_____

_____

BE AN OPEN BOOK
LET LIFE HAPPEN THROUGHOUT YOU
SO OTHERS WILL SEE

OCTOBER 26

HAVE TIME MANAGEMENT
BE PRODUCTIVE WITH YOUR TIME
AND ACCOMPLISH MORE

OCTOBER 27

_____

_____

_____

_____

_____

_____

_____

_____

_____

_____

DO NOT LET LOSING
KEEP YOU FROM PLAYING THE GAME
BE VICTORIOUS

OCTOBER 28

_____

_____

_____

_____

_____

_____

_____

_____

_____

_____

_____

_____

SEIZE EVERY MOMENT
DO WHAT YOU WANT TO DO NOW
NEVER HAVE REGRET

OCTOBER 29

_____

_____

_____

_____

_____

_____

_____

_____

_____

_____

LIVING OUT YOUR DREAMS
CAN BECOME SCARY AT TIMES
BUT IT'S WORTH THE RISK

OCTOBER 30

THERE IS NO SUCH THING
AS A STUPID QUESTION OR
CRAZY IDEA

OCTOBER 31

NEVER BE AFRAID
TO FACE THE IMPOSSIBLE
ELIMINATE FEAR

NOVEMBER 1

_____

_____

_____

_____

_____

_____

_____

_____

_____

_____

_____

_____

YOU MUST MAKE THE TIME
FOR THINGS IMPORTANT TO YOU
EVERY SINGLE DAY

NOVEMBER 2

_____

_____

_____

_____

_____

_____

_____

_____

_____

_____

HAPPINESS CAN NOT
BE FAR BEHIND A STRONG HEART
AND A PEACEFUL MIND

NOVEMBER 3

_____

_____

_____

_____

_____

_____

_____

_____

_____

_____

_____

TREAT YOURSELF AS YOU
WOULD LIKE OTHERS TO TREAT YOU
EACH AND EVERY DAY

NOVEMBER 4

_____

_____

_____

_____

_____

_____

_____

_____

_____

_____

ALWAYS BE THANKFUL
GIVING THANKS IS EASY FOR
EVERYONE TO DO

NOVEMBER 5

_____

_____

_____

_____

_____

_____

_____

_____

_____

_____

_____

THERE WILL ALWAYS BE
SOMETHING TO BE THANKFUL FOR
IN EVERYONE'S LIFE

NOVEMBER 6

_____

_____

_____

_____

_____

_____

_____

_____

_____

_____

BE INSPIRED BY YOUR
DAILY STRUGGLES AND WORK TO
MAKE A BETTER YOU

NOVEMBER 7

_____

_____

_____

_____

_____

_____

_____

_____

_____

_____

_____

KNOW YOUR TRUE WORTH AND
LIVE EACH DAY TO THE FULLEST
BY GIVING YOUR BEST

NOVEMBER 8

GIVE THANKS TO OTHERS
ALWAYS SHOW YOUR GRATITUDE
APPRECIATION

NOVEMBER 9

DO SOMETHING TODAY
AND MAKE SOMEONE SHOW THEIR SMILE
SO OTHERS CAN SEE

NOVEMBER 10

_____

WAKE UP GET GOING
LIVE OUT EACH DAY WORRY FREE
FOCUS ON TODAY

NOVEMBER 11

_____

_____

_____

_____

_____

_____

_____

_____

_____

_____

_____

_____

HELP A VETERAN
ALWAYS SHOW THEM YOUR SUPPORT
BY SAYING THANK YOU

NOVEMBER 12

SHARE YOUR EXPERIENCE
IT CAN BRING HOPE TO OTHERS
AND HELP INSPIRE THEM

NOVEMBER 13

_____

_____

_____

_____

_____

_____

_____

_____

_____

_____

_____

WHEN LIFE STARTS TO GET
INCREDIBLY DIFFICULT
PRAY AND ASK FOR HELP

NOVEMBER 14

YOU'RE NEVER ALONE
IF YOU HAVE GOOD FRIENDS AND A
LOVING FAMILY

NOVEMBER 15

_____

_____

_____

_____

_____

_____

_____

_____

_____

_____

_____

WHAT EVER OCCURS
DO NOT LET THINGS STOP YOU FROM
ACHIEVING YOUR DREAMS

NOVEMBER 16

_____

_____

_____

_____

_____

_____

_____

_____

_____

_____

_____

BE INSPIRED BY YOUR
DAILY STRUGGLES AND WORK TO
MAKE A BETTER YOU

NOVEMBER 17

PACE YOURSELF IN LIFE
DO NOT GET BURNED OUT CHASING
THE WAYS OF THE WORLD

NOVEMBER 18

_____

_____

_____

_____

_____

_____

_____

_____

_____

_____

BE A ROLE MODEL

PEOPLE LOOK UP TO OTHERS

TO SHOW THEM THE WAY

NOVEMBER 19

_____

_____

_____

_____

_____

_____

_____

_____

_____

_____

_____

_____

DON'T TAKE LIFE FOR GRANTED
IT CAN BE TAKEN AWAY
WITHIN AN INSTANT

NOVEMBER 20

WAKE UP EACH DAY AND
BE THANKFUL FOR EVERYTHING
YOU HAVE IN YOUR LIFE

NOVEMBER 21

_____

_____

_____

_____

_____

_____

_____

_____

_____

_____

BE THANKFUL ALWAYS
BE HAPPY WITH THE SMALL THINGS
IN YOUR LIFE TODAY

NOVEMBER 22

_____

_____

_____

_____

_____

_____

_____

_____

_____

_____

PUT YOUR LOVE ONE'S FIRST
SPENDING TIME WITH FAMILY
SHOWS THEM THAT YOU CARE

NOVEMBER 23

HAVE A THANKFUL HEART
APPRECIATE THE SMALL THINGS
YOUR BLESSINGS WILL COME

NOVEMBER 24

_____

_____

_____

_____

_____

_____

_____

_____

_____

_____

MAKE GREAT MEMORIES
THROUGHOUT EVERY HOLIDAY
WITH YOUR FAMILY

NOVEMBER 25

DON'T CALL IT A DREAM
BUT CALL IT A SOLID PLAN
PUT INTO MOTION

NOVEMBER 26

_____

_____

_____

_____

_____

_____

_____

_____

_____

_____

_____

DO NOT JUDGE YOUR PAST
YOU NO LONGER LIVE THERE SO
LOOK AT YOUR FUTURE

NOVEMBER 27

_____

_____

_____

_____

_____

_____

_____

_____

_____

_____

_____

START YOUR DAY OFF RIGHT
BY MAKING A SOLID PLAN
AND SEE YOUR GOALS THROUGH

NOVEMBER 28

Always be thankful
For waking up again to
See another day

NOVEMBER 29

_____

_____

_____

_____

_____

_____

_____

_____

_____

_____

TELL YOUR FRIENDS THANK YOU
FOR EVERYTHING THAT THEY'VE DONE
AND FOR BEING THERE

NOVEMBER 30

DON'T ALLOW YOURSELF
TO QUIT WORKING ON YOUR GOALS
WHEN LIFE GETS TOO HARD

DECEMBER 1

Have faith in yourself
Never stop believing that
You are meant for more

DECEMBER 2

_____

_____

_____

_____

_____

_____

_____

_____

_____

_____

ALWAYS LOVE YOURSELF
LOVE AND RESPECT ALL WOMEN
AND HELP YOUR ELDERS

DECEMBER 3

Always be joyful
Be the person that others
Seek when things are down

DECEMBER 4

LIFE IS NOT PERFECT
IT WILL TEST AND CHALLENGE YOUR
WILL AND STRENGTH EACH DAY

DECEMBER 5

_____

_____

_____

_____

_____

_____

_____

_____

_____

_____

WHY TRY TO FIT IN
YOU WERE BORN TO STAND OUT AND
MAKE A DIFFERENCE

DECEMBER 6

_____

_____

_____

_____

_____

_____

_____

_____

_____

_____

_____

SHARE WHAT YOU HAVE LEARNED
IT MAY HELP AND BENEFIT
SOMEONE ELSE EACH DAY

DECEMBER 7

_____

_____

_____

_____

_____

_____

_____

_____

_____

_____

_____

_____

ALWAYS TELL THE TRUTH

LYING BRINGS PAIN AND HEARTACHE

ALWAYS BE TRUTHFUL

DECEMBER 8

_____

_____

_____

_____

_____

_____

_____

_____

_____

_____

ALWAYS BE GIVING
OF YOUR TIME TO HELP OTHERS
EVERY CHANCE YOU GET

DECEMBER 9

_____

_____

_____

_____

_____

_____

_____

_____

_____

_____

KNOW HOW TO EXCEED
AND BE SUCCESSFUL IN LIFE
SHOW YOUR WOW FACTOR

DECEMBER 10

_____

_____

_____

_____

_____

_____

_____

_____

_____

_____

BECOME PASSIONATE
BE ENGAGED IN EVERYTHING
AND LOVE WHAT YOU DO

DECEMBER 11

ALWAYS HAVE RESPECT
FOR EVERYONE AROUND YOU
AND EXPECT IT BACK

DECEMBER 12

_____

_____

_____

_____

_____

_____

_____

_____

_____

_____

ACCOMPLISH YOURSELF
USE YOUR ABILITY AND
DON'T ACCEPT DEFEAT

DECEMBER 13

Always remember
That people are beautiful
Both inside and out

DECEMBER 14

EVERY SINGLE DAY
SHOW UNCONDITIONAL LOVE
CONNECT WITH OTHERS

DECEMBER 15

HAVE A CARING HEART
COMPASSION LIVES IN YOU
ALWAYS EMBRACE IT

DECEMBER 16

DO NOT BE STUBBORN
YOUR FINAL DESTINATION
HAS NOT BEEN SET YET

DECEMBER 17

_____

_____

_____

_____

_____

_____

_____

_____

_____

_____

_____

USING GOOD MANNERS
SHOULD BE A REQUIREMENT NOT
AN OBLIGATION

DECEMBER 18

LISTEN CAREFULLY
ALWAYS PAY ATTENTION AND
ACKNOWLEDGE OTHERS

DECEMBER 19

Remain positive
Don't let negative people
Tear you down in life

DECEMBER 20

_____

_____

_____

_____

_____

_____

_____

_____

_____

_____

_____

SMILE AND BE HAPPY
GREET EVERYONE AROUND YOU
MAKE SOMEONE'S DAY GREAT

DECEMBER 21

_____

_____

_____

_____

_____

_____

_____

_____

_____

_____

_____

DO NOT LET WINTER
SLOW YOU DOWN OR STOP YOU COLD
FROM PLANNING WHAT'S NEXT

DECEMBER 22

_____

_____

_____

_____

_____

_____

_____

_____

_____

_____

DO NOT WASTE YOUR HEART
LOVE DOESN'T TAKE A HOLIDAY
SO NEITHER SHOULD YOU

DECEMBER 23

_____

_____

_____

_____

_____

_____

_____

_____

_____

_____

NEVER CHANGE SOMEONE
LOVE PEOPLE FOR WHO THEY ARE
SHOW THEM COMPASSION

DECEMBER 24

_____

_____

_____

_____

_____

_____

_____

_____

_____

_____

_____

PUTTING OTHERS FIRST
BETTER TO GIVE THAN RECEIVE
ALWAYS SHOW KINDNESS

DECEMBER 25

CHRISTMAS DAY IS HERE
DON'T FORGET THE TRUE REASON
FOR THIS YEAR'S SEASON

DECEMBER 26

_____

_____

_____

_____

_____

_____

_____

_____

_____

_____

SHOWING AND GIVING
LOVE SHOULD BE DISPLAYED DAILY
NOT JUST HOLIDAYS

DECEMBER 27

Make others smile today
Kind words last forever so
Be true to yourself

DECEMBER 28

CHANGE YOUR THOUGHT PROCESS
STEP OUT OF YOUR COMFORT ZONE
AND TRANSFORM YOUR LIFE

DECEMBER 29

_____

_____

_____

_____

_____

_____

_____

_____

_____

_____

_____

START PLANNING AHEAD
YOUR FUTURE IS CREATED
BY YOUR DAILY THOUGHTS

DECEMBER 30

DON'T KEEP LOOKING BACK
YOU WILL NEVER NOTICE WHAT
LIES AHEAD FOR YOU

DECEMBER 31

_____

_____

_____

_____

_____

_____

_____

_____

_____

_____

_____

LET GO OF REGRETS
PUT A PLAN INTO PLACE TO
START THE NEW YEAR RIGHT!

ABOUT THE AUTHOR

Geoffrey Foose is a social worker at a local healthcare facility. Geoffrey attended and earned a degree in Psychology from the University of Central Florida. The author was inspired by changing events in his own life to write this collection of poems (quotes). It is his desire that this book will encourage you to move forward each day and live out your passion. Geoffrey, author of The Leap Forward lives in Virginia Beach, Virginia with his three children

Printed in the United States
By Bookmasters